THE ECONOMICS OF DOLLARIZATION AND MONEY SUPPLY

A simple primer to economic manipulation and wealth concentration

© Copyright rests with the author

This book is a matter of perspective and opinion. It does not purport to represent an expert view on economics or any other discipline. It is based on observation and inferences.

Any references to people, organizations and situations are intended to explain a point of view and should not be construed as opinions on the efficacy of the people or organizations involved. Every part of this book is a perspective and opinion and does not always purport to represent facts. Research required to ascertain every fact, especially in situations where facts are reported differently depending on who is being asked, has not been exhaustively undertaken. This book is not a result of academic research and should be viewed accordingly.

No part of this book may be copied, re-published, re-produced or otherwise transmitted without the express permission of the author.

John Dixon is a pen name of the author. Any communication with the author may be made to kdppublish@gmail.com.

Version 1.0 - Created in April 2021

Prologue

THE RICH WILL GET RICHER

THE POOR WILL GET POORER

THE DOLLAR REMAINS KING

EVERYTHING GETS CONSUMED OR HOARDED BEFORE IT TRICKLES DOWN

CENTRAL BANKS ARE KEY TO STRENGTHENING THE ILLUSION THAT THERE EXISTS BALANCE AND INTEGRITY IN FINANCIAL MARKETS

Economics has long been an art sold as a science. Fancy graphs and equations that are supposed to make everyone believe that somebody knows what's going on. That somebody is in control. That some monetary or fiscal policy and its execution are somehow going to benefit the average working person. Economics cannot be a science because a science requires a determinate outcome. Economics has never given a determinate outcome. Economics could at best be called at art. But not the art you are thinking it is.

Economics is the art of trickery, deceit and sleight of hand. A good economist is a magician who makes you believe in the illusion, astounds you with words, numbers and theories and finally leaves you gaping. Not gaping at the trick, itself but gaping at yourself for not having understood why you are still not rich. Then there are the mediocre economists. The wannabe magicians who would explain everything in hindsight. The ones who will explain to you why and only if you had done something, you would have been here or there. One wonders if such foresight is demonstrated in hindsight, why is the person revealing the trick not rich himself/ herself.

Economics can be divided into two distinct types – the ones who make policy (create the illusion) and the ones who explain the illusion (the commentators). The irony is that neither really has a clue what the cause and effect of anything is on a macro scale. The only difference between the illusionist and the explainer is that the illusionist has the power to reinforce the illusion of fair markets and control. Not reinforce this illusion through actions or policy but by words and random data sets. Words and random data sets that perceivably move markets and make the average working person believe he/ she is the only one not understanding how a perfect system works.

WHEN A SYSTEM IS SO GOOD THAT ONLY 1% OF THE PEOPLE PRETEND TO UNDERSTAND IT, THE OTHER 99% ARE BEING LIED TO.

Now, no argument on economics is complete without asking whether socialism is better or capitalism. That argument can now be extended to whether autocracy is better for economic well being or democracy. The simple answer is that it doesn't matter. A philosophy or system is as good as the people enforcing it. Whether socialism, capitalism or any other prism defines economics, the results won't be very different. The arguments for or against socialism and capitalism are merely an attempt by the illusionists and commentators to keep the illusion alive. Another data point that makes no sense to the larger population but is deemed right because the illusion is still alive.

Economics finally comes down to two things alone: money supply and dollarization. Money supply is how central banks continue to exercise control by creating an asset or an illusion of its availability. The asset itself is backed by virtually nothing other than the paper it is printed on. Yet the asset becomes valuable as it continues to be sought after. Imagine a situation where somebody told you they are regulating the supply of air you breathe because they said there must be enough for everyone. Then, they increase or decrease the supply with some justification. As a result, some people choke and die, and some survive. What's worse is imagine where that air is unevenly distributed; allowing some to die and some to survive. Every day you are gasping for air to breathe and hoping the air supply continues. Now imagine if you realize that the person controlling the air supply could at any point provide more air depending on their "policy". That extra provision of air makes you happy, but do you question why you couldn't have the air in the first place. Money supply is pretty much like that. Central banks can decide how much to print and who gets how much of the printed money. Who lives off the money, who dies because they didn't get enough and who keeps getting a trickle amount? The balancing act is very simple. The illusion almost so simple that it hides in plain sight. As long as people are focussed on getting their trickle and continue to struggle for it, they will ignore the fact that there are others inordinately benefited by central bank policies. As long as the ones who die because they didn't get enough are hidden from plain sight by moving them to institutions, shelters or other places away from the broader society; and this is reinforced by dropping poverty numbers, which are conveniently driven by where the poverty line is drawn and not purchasing power, the 99% will keep struggling on, gasping for their little share of air for survival. The illusion is that the central bank and monetary policy through control of inflation is helping you. In reality, it is simply regulating money supply and leaving you gasping for survival.

THE THEORY OF MONEY SUPPLY HAS LONG BEEN CHAMPIONED AS THE ULTIMATE EQUILIBRIUM IN MACRO ECONOMICS. IN REALITY, IT IS THE ROOT CAUSE OF THE EVER-EXPANDING DIVIDE BETWEEN THE RICH AND THE POOR.

The other major anchor factor in economics is dollarization. Now, one may argue that dollarization is not a global phenomenon. Central banks and governments around the world will swear, they have nothing to do with dollarization. Dollarization, though, is the bedrock of expansionary economics. It is the mother of all money supply illusions. Let's understand how. When central banks printed currency earlier, they kept gold or silver or some asset that justified the printing of currency. In simple terms, if someone turned up with a currency note, which is basically an IOU note that the central bank has issued, the central bank would be obliged to give them an equivalent amount of gold. Then started the first step of the deceit. Central banks or governments were free to fix exchange rates between gold and the printed currency, thereby transferring their deficits and debts to unsuspecting holders of currency. Simply put, central banks could decide that the 10 dollars they borrowed from you against a guarantee of gold would now cost 20 dollars for you to buy back that gold. This was a simple way to transfer the burden of deficit from the government to the people.

Then came the second step of the deceit. Why keep gold while printing currency? All you had to do was abolish the gold standard. Tell people that they can keep the currency and they wouldn't get the gold back if they presented the IOU note. Basically, ensuring that the money would never be taken out of circulation and could never seek back a real asset. This also meant that central banks could recklessly print currency and then jointly with the government could decide through monetary policy, fiscal stimulus, subsidies and investments who got access to the recklessly printed money. People with abundant access to this money bought and held real assets and borrowed even more through low interest rate regimes. The average common man was told the importance of savings and he religiously held onto the cash under his/ her mattress or in bank accounts that paid interest rates lower than inflation. Everyday, the average common man's money was depreciating in value as more money was printed and he had no ability to buy high value assets or was constrained from borrowing due to perceived credit worthiness. Now, this little perfect illusion worked brilliantly in closed economies. It helped the creation and rise of the blue-blooded families who for generations stayed rich because of assets created through preferential access to money supply.

Then came the little problem called global trade. Cash printed by central banks in one country did not hold the same value in another country. So, there were only two ways to keep the illusion going as people travelled and traded with other countries. The final deceit: dollarization. Dollarization happened when central banks agreed that they could settle their obligations in another country's currency by exchanging it for a third currency instead of gold. The most preferred currency became the US Dollar. Now, dollarization took two forms. Some countries fuelled the deceit through currency pegs against the dollar thereby allowing them to manipulate the relative value of their currency. Other chose to float against the US Dollar. The result was the same. Central banks continued their sleight of hand controlling who got their hands on the money supply. Dollarization is defined by the IMF as follows: "Dollarization, the holding by residents of a significant share of their assets in the form of foreign-currency-denominated assets, is a common feature of developing countries and transition economies and is thereby typical--to a greater or lesser extent--of many countries that have IMF-supported adjustment programs." In simple terms, the people who now had access to money supply could own assets not just in-country but globally, further expanding their wealth. And the 99% in-country could join the ranks of the other 99% globally in gawking at the illusion. Dollarization also gave the Federal Reserve the leeway to print as much as they wanted by a convenient measure called buying of US Treasuries by the Federal Reserve. Simply put, the Federal Reserve funds the US Government while the US and global working class sees the value of their money fall as their money is worth less and less relative to the value of hard and financial assets. Of course, the fiscal and monetary programs of the US Government supported by interest rate cuts, fiscal stimulus packages, corporate tax cuts, subsidies and co-investments help ensure that money supply remains with the 1% blue blooded. The addition to the ranks of the blue blooded by those touted as tech entrepreneurs are simply a fraction of the people who have been able to tap into financial asset valuation by monetizing financial holdings in their own enterprises. A small window of opportunity for the 99% to get access to the money routed to and destined for the blue bloods.

DOLLARIZATION ONLY STRENGTENS THE GLOBAL POSITION OF THE CRONY CAPITALISTS – THE BLUE BLOODS. BLUE BLOODS ARE NOT ASTUTE BUSINESSMEN BUT ASTUTE THIEFS WHO STEAL THE MONEY BEFORE IT TRICKLES DOWN. THE GREEDIER THE BLUE BLOODS IN THE SYSTEM, THE LESS THE MONEY TRICKLES DOWN.

The economics of dollarization and money supply have created a large irrevocable imbalance in society. A society where people are not rewarded for hard work, intelligence, or aptitude. But are rewarded for crony capitalism. Crony capitalism exists in every state – socialist or capitalist, autocratic or democratic. Dispelling the economics of dollarization and money supply is possible only through a fundamental dismantling of the central banking system, rewriting the rules of global trade and more importantly accountability of fiscal spending and programs down to the last cent. The irony of accountability is that businesses and individuals are required to account for every last cent in their tax returns and through their published financials. Governments and central banks are allowed to not provide account of how they have created bluebloods who serve to help them retain power and help them keep control over the 99%.

While cryptocurrencies and other forms of digital currencies seeking to replace the central banking system threaten the system, their varying approaches and sometimes own imbalances have prevented wider adoption. This is coupled with the crack down by governments and central banks themselves. Dismantling and re-assembling the system will take a lot more than vain attempts at cryptos.

CRYPTOS DO NOT TAKE THE BULL BY THE HORNS BY SIMPLY TRYING TO CREATE AN ALTERNATE MEDIUM OF EXCHANGE. IN THEIR CURRENT FORM AND TRAJECTORY, CRYPTOS WILL ALSO GET DOLLARIZED.

Now for the biggest economic deceit of all – interest rates. Economics has always been taught as a function of demand and supply. If you have more of something, it will be worth lesser and vice versa. So, if you have more of money, it should yield lesser interest rates and vice versa. Sounds good in theory and should work perfectly by re-adjusting automatically the value of money. Well, no. The central banks who print money also set interest rates. The one who prints an illusionary asset also sets its price. More so, central banks are regular interest and currency rate manipulators, and this holds true without exception. By themselves trading in bond markets, buying and selling government securities and setting policy rates, they decide what the price of the asset should be. So, central banks not just control your access to the money. They also decide that, if you have saved some money or need money, how much it is worth. Not free market forces as told to you. Without exception, whether in socialist or capitalist economics, free market forces do not decide the value of your money. Central banks do.

ECONOMICS IS THE TOOL THAT CONTROLS 99% OF THE POPULATION. IT IS NEITHER AN ART NOR A SCIENCE. IT IS MERELY A TOOL OF DECEIT JUSTIFIED BY LARGE WORDS AND MOSTLY BASELESS THEORIES.

CHAPTER 1
HOW THE RICH GET RICHER

Chapter 1 – How the rich get richer

For many centuries, the rich have become richer by humouring the kings and rulers of old. The underlying premise has remained the same. However, the methods have become more sophisticated – complicated by the needs of hypocrisy that accompanies democracy. The principle for centuries has been the same – money does not give you true power. True power is earned by force or by manipulating the minds of the masses. The rulers do not seek to amass wealth. They only seek to amass as much as is required to help them retain power. The wealth must then be unequally distributed to cronies – people who shall do the biding of the state. The power of its distribution should, however, be retained by the rulers.

In the good old days, where hypocrisy was not as prevalent or needed, the simple method of wealth allocation would be granting a person land, rights to business, the ability collect tax or the ability to plunder without consequences. Such methods, though vile, were quite effective in creating and retaining a power structure that ensured continuity in ruling and ensured retention of power with the crown, the king or the czar. The peasants who spoke against the power structure were crushed by anyone in the power structure and the state condoned such extra judicial killing in the name of preventing sedition. History is littered with stories of poor peasants oppressed and destitute as every word against any part of the power structure was met with stiff retribution.

The power structure would have survived and thrived if only the power structures were non-intersecting Venn diagrams. The peasant would have had no chance and the kings would have continued to rule. However, with power comes a greater innate human weakness – greed which is further exacerbated by ego. The power structures went to war with each other seeking to expand their empires. With each passing moment, they continued to make the rich richer by giving them contracts to equip the wars. The contracts to equip wars later turned into funding of the war by the elite and crony capitalists. Such funding of war made the state indebted and weakened it financially. However, it boosted the ego of the kings and ensured that the crony capitalists kept being fed for generations. The crony capitalists on their part ensured succession of the kingdoms so that the policies continued. The peasants every now and then saw a ray of hope with a just king. However, the deep-rooted system was never going to be uprooted.

As the kingdoms fought on, new philosophies emerged – democracy and communism. Both were seen as methods to return power to the people. The crony capitalists resisted but the writing on the wall was clear. The wild wild west comprising of exiles was going to overthrow the system. It would be replaced by democracy and capitalism in its true naked form. Democracy would be sold as the will of the people, but it would merely distribute power from one king to many small kings – people who would ostensibly be elected representatives of the people. In reality, they would be men and women instated into places of power through money that funded their campaigns. Campaign money and lobbying would soon become the norm of the new democratic world order where people instated by the people would deceive the people by drawing out policies and awarding lucrative contracts to the same blue bloods who excelled under the kings of old.

As the world wars raged on and the kingdoms were weakened making way for democracy, there rose another philosophy. That of communism, a philosophy that promised to return power to the people and strip away naked capitalism. Communism was not allowed to flourish in most democracies as it was deemed anti-freedom. It was labelled a way of life that would destroy economies. More importantly it was a way of life that would shake the world order of crony capitalists of old. The problem with communism did not lie with its philosophy but by it being coupled with autocracy. The implementation of communism was predicated on the belief that the people do not know better than the state. The state in turn would be select group of people appointed in much the same way as the kings of old. If anything, communism, where coupled with autocracy would prove to reinforce crony capitalism in ways that even the kings of old didn't manage. Communism would eventually die its natural death, but autocracy would live on in the communist countries of old.

COMMUNISM AND CAPITALISM ARE TWO SIDES TO THE SAME ECONOMIC EQUATION OF MAINTAINING THE IMABALANCE OF WEALTH DISTRIBUTION. NEITHER SEEKS TO BALANCE AN IMBALANCED EQUATION. BOTH ONLY WEIGH IN ON OPPOSITE SIDES OF THE EQUATION.

Communism was propagated by the soldiers of the erstwhile kings as they saw both the kings power slip away and their utility diminish as democracies took over. Communism, in its true sense, was a vain attempt by the fighting class or hired mercenaries of the kings to let the old order live on. The peasants who ostensibly supported their movements where promised greater good and more equity only to be fooled time and time again as the power transfer was completed.

COMMUNISM IS THE GOVERNMENT OF THE AUTOCRATS, FOR THE CRONY CAPITALISTS AND BY THE MISGUDED PEOPLE WHO ARE TEMPTED BY PHILOSOPHIES AND SHORT-TERM GAINS PROMISED AT THE BEGINNING OF EACH REVOLUTION.

DEMOCRACY COUPLED WITH CAPITALISM IN ITS CURRENT FORM IS THE GOVERNMENT OF THE HYPOCRITES, BY THE PEOPLE AND FOR THE CRONY CAPITALISTS

Yet, while years of social change coupled with infinite wars played out, one thing remained constant, the rich fortified their wealth. The few rich who lost out fell afoul of the system due to gambling or crime. Fast forward to the system today. The system today world over almost without exception makes the rich richer and poor poorer. So, how does it work exactly.

The kingdoms of today continue to operate in exactly the same way. A network of families given ministries by the kings and rulers coupled with exploitation of natural resources. Where communism exists, it has become more potent than the communism of old. It is now capitalist autocracy not communist autocracy. The worst of both forms of economic system coupled together to ensure naked allocation of wealth to those preferred by the ruling class. The ruling class now takes the form of single party systems, politburos and sometimes even a sham parliament. All these capitalist autocracies have a front face called a President sometimes a Prime Minister and sometimes vanity names like Supreme Leader. Yet, all operate in the same manner. They keep the peasants at bay through policies and state sponsored controls that enable the rich to accumulate great wealth quietly and suavely. These leaders are a lot swifter to shut down dissent even where such dissent occurs from within the crony capitalists. Lessons learnt from the past by these new rulers have taught them to crush dissent before it becomes a movement. They also understand that the peasants, irrespective of their occupation today, are easily swayed away by dissenting voices which must be crushed before they reach the peasants and start a new revolution. The economics of the kingdoms and the ruling communists differ only slightly. The kingdoms redistribute national wealth to their supporters whereas the communists seek to steal global wealth and redistribute it to the few they sponsor.

Stealing global wealth by communists is simple yet practical. They steal intellectual property, deal in intelligence, engage in intellectual property piracy, manipulate currencies and simply extort through kidnapping. All this is sold to the peasants as betterment of the state – love of the motherland, fatherland or homeland. Yet, it never reaches the peasants. It is a scheme of stealing from the rich to give to the rich.

AUTOCRATIC CAPITALIST COMMUNISTS ARE GLOBAL THIEFS THAT OPERATE ON A MASSIVE AND UNPRECENDETED SCALE. THEY SIMPLY SEEK TOE REDISTRIBUTE POWER TO PEOPLE THEY SPONSOR TO PROTECT THEMSLEVES FROM OUTSIDE FORCES. THEY ARE THE NEW AGE ROBINHOODS WHO STEAL FROM THE RICH AND GIVE TO THE RICH.

Now before you start thinking that democratic capitalism is the holy grail, take a pause. Democratic capitalism in its current form operates under no different premise. It seeks to steal from the poor and give to the rich. And this it achieves through the economics of money supply. The economics of money supply are a simple yet grand theft. It works on the premise that the one creating the asset can appreciate or depreciate an asset merely by their actions. They can then transfer that asset to the ones they choose, who can in turn change the holding form of that asset to benefit from such appreciation or depreciation. The ones who don't have insight into this hold the wrong asset and get burnt. Now if this sounds all very complicated, lets simplify that.

DEMOCRACTIC CAPITALISM IN ITS CURRENT FORM IS A MECHANISM OF STEALING FROM THE POOR AND GIVING TO THE RICH BY LEGIMITZING ASSET VALUE MAINPULATIONS BY THE GOVERNMENT OR CENTRAL BANKS.

The economics of money supply work in a very simple manner:
- The central bank prints currency

- The central bank uses the currency to buy bonds issued by the government
- The central bank sets interest rates or rather fixes interest rates
- The government continues to borrow recklessly to funds its many programs
- The programs the government funds are those that effectively place money in the hands of the crony capitalists either through direct benefit transfers or through tax breaks or by just awarding them high value government contracts
- The crony capitalists access the money and use it to buy assets
- The crony capitalists then leverage these assets to buy more assets
- The assets then inflate in value as more money chases few assets
- The poor people then invest in these assets when the bubble is at its largest
- The central banks then reign in money supply and make it expensive by increasing interest rates
- The poor people who have invested in assets like homes see their interest rates rise and start defaulting as they can't afford the assets
- The crony capitalists by this time have dumped the assets and are sitting on liquidity
- They then use this liquidity to buy assets cheap
- If the crony capitalists get the timing wrong and are caught on the wrong side of liquidity or credit risk, the government prepares a bailout package under the garb of saving jobs
- The printed money then refills the coffers of the crony capitalists
- The poor barely get a smidgen of the bailout money and become poorer than they were and even debt ridden
- The poor who didn't buy assets and sat of money see the value of their money depreciate as reckless printing creates more inflation
- This cycle continues and each such cycle makes the rich richer and the poor poorer

EACH ECONOMIC CYCLE IN DEMOCRACTIC CAPITALISM IS THE START OF NEW RICHES BEING CREATED FOR THE EXISTING

RICH. THE END OF EACH ECONOMIC CYCLE IS MARKED WITH BAILOUTS FOR THE SAME RICH. THE POOR ARE MERELY SPECTATORS AS THEIR WEALTH DWINDLES.

Now let's address the detractors because each point raises questions as to how does such a system work so beautifully and the poor keep getting fooled. So, let's answer the detractors before we move forward.

- *Why can't the poor also exercise as much intelligence as the rich and buy assets early in the cycle?*

  The answer is simple – the rich have access to credit that the poor don't. Access to credit is dependent not on strong underwriting skills of banks but based on existing asset holdings, family name, collateral, political influence and in most cases allowing the banks to share in the pie of the scam called the economics of money supply. The poor have no such ability or access to collateral to make deals with the banks and buy in early. They buy in late because banks prey on their weakness at the late stage of the cycle and take advantage of their human desire to also participate in the upside with the rich people.

- *The economics of money supply are self-balancing. Money supply and interest rates are inversely related.*

  This presumption would hold true if and only if the supply of money was not controlled by the same entity setting interest rates. Imagine a situation where there is only shop in town and this shop has an unlimited supply of food. This shop decides when to sell it cheap and when to sell it expensive. More importantly, this shop decides whom to give it to cheap and whom to give it to expensive. Central banks decide in the same way that money should be priced differently for different people. They print the money and then allow banks to access it cheaply. These banks in turn supply it cheap to whom they want under the garb of credit risk. So, in simple terms the central banks control both the access to money and the price of money i.e. interest rates. The equation is never self-balancing. The equation is balanced by a forced reset that the central banks undertake at the point of the cycle most convenient for the rich.

- *The government runs a huge deficit to support the poor and provide infrastructure. The central bank is merely funding the needs of the poor.*

The great eyewash called taxes is the government making people pay for what they consume. Now the reality is that the government through both indirect and direct taxes earns more than enough to ensure that services are provided to its citizens. Yet, it does not provide these services and offloads their responsibility to the private sector. The private sector aka crony capitalists then charge the poor people exorbitant amounts of people to provide them services for which they have paid taxes in the first place. The government then gets more money printed by the central bank to provide handouts to the rich and the members of itself thereby enriching itself further. So, the average working person pays taxes and gets less in return and then loses the value of his/ her savings as the central bank prints more money.

- *The quality of life has improved, and people are consuming more nowadays. Every person is better off.*

People are consuming more from borrowed money. As they keep consuming, crony capitalists keep making money and banks keep seeing their balance sheets fatten. Consumer debt has grown disproportionately to increase in consumption. It only means that the average person is being provided debt to meet his/ her consumption needs and to not create assets. Having a base case increase in consumption and equating that with a better quality of life is one the greatest fallacies of economics. Higher consumption does not mean better quality of life. It merely means higher GDP and similar metrics that determine the value added in the economy. Value added to whom is the quintessential question – and the answer is value added to the rich.

- *There are people who have broken out and become rich.*

That is true. There are people who have broken out. There are four ways to break-out (i) crime (ii) speculation if you are lucky (iii) becoming a crony capitalist yourself (iv) genius in varying proportions. Now, unless you join the club, become a criminal or get lucky, you are relying on your genius to break out. Genius in varying degrees that has created the tech billionaires and millionaires of this era. However, their numbers in comparison to the larger population are a dip in the ocean. Also, these people who have broken out continue to be demonized by the political class by propagating conspiracy theories around data privacy and some such. The question one must ask if how much more data have governments sold or just given to private enterprises in the name of credit scoring and background checks? And yet, they demonize the people who seek to break free through genius. Make no mistake, these tech entrepreneurs are not beyond reproach in their ways. But the people who demonize them seek only to restore the old order and have no goodwill at heart.

All this does beg the question. Isn't communist autocracy then better than capitalist democracy since it steals from the rich and gives to the rich? That isn't true because it is simply a matter of time. As the rich from whom the communists steal either dwindle or become smarter and stop the stealing, the communists will turn to the poor again. They will use tools they have used for generations again which include higher taxation to the point of and including after death, extorting in the name of fines for small infractions, nationalizing property ownership or simply going to war to steal some more. A communist autocracy works on an unbalanced equation. Sooner or later, it must either succumb or consume others. A capitalist democracy, however unfair, works on an equation that is balanced by central banks through the economics of money supply. Increasingly, the communist autocracies and the kingdoms have realized that this is the key to sustainability. The economics of money supply are being perfected by these autocratic states as they increasingly understand that stealing from the poor consistently and sneakily is far easier than stealing from the rich or stealing from the poor through extortion.

THE CONVERGENCE OF THE EONOMICS OF MONEY SUPPLY BETWEEN DEMOCRACTIC CAPITALISM, AUTOCRACTIC COMMUNISM AND KINGDOMS CREATES AN ALMOST UNIVERSAL ORDER THAT IS INDISTINGUISHABLE. THE WORLD ORDER FURTHER CEMENTS AND ENHANCES THE GAP BETWEEN THE RICH AND THE POOR.

CHAPTER 2
HOW THE POOR GET POORER

Chapter 2 – How the poor get poorer

The poor get poorer in many small ways. However, there are two primary things that keep the poor poor and make them poorer – (i) education (ii) savings. Now before you think this is cuckoo let mulls over why.

Education has long been touted as the way to uplift people from poverty. The only avenue towards freedom and a dignified life. While this is not entirely untrue and it has uplifted people from poverty, it has done only that much. Helped eradicate or reduce poverty. It hasn't made people any less poor. Now to understand the difference between poor and poverty, it is important to understand that there is no universal definition of poor. Many a times, philosophers will tell you that poverty is a state of mind. It definitely is a state of mind, just not that of the poor person but the blue bloods who decide what that state shall be. Poverty is the state of utter uselessness to the state. A state that can lead to civil unrest and social ills that break the very backbone of the state and maybe even start a revolution. Poor is a state of living within very limited means, a single income and small savings that largely help the heirs of the saving member. Now, one may say that education is uplifting and that is true. It uplifts you from poverty to being poor and then it caps your upliftment. It ensures that you join the workforce – a group of people paid wages sufficient to keep them indifferent to the ways of the state and the manner in which their wealth is plundered by the crony capitalists. One may say this is the price the poor pay for peace. An ultimate extortion by the state and its cronies. Education has been created as a pre-requisite for most jobs – not skill but education. This virtually ensures that in most countries people are employable until they attain 21 years of age.

Over the last few decades, education has, in some cases, proved more uplifting that transitioning a person from poverty to just poor. Certain high paying careers and sometimes businesses have resulted from education that was provided as a service by the state in return for taxes. It was, therefore, time to change the rules of the game. The blue bloods simply made education expensive through the same old route called privatization. The quality of state provided education continued to diminish and access to such education remained limited to the very few. The very few first determined by merit and then determined by their parents' ability to donate or add to endowments. The rich then funded universities or created new universities, colleges and other forms of education. These means of education were well funded and created a new standard in imparting knowledge. They held and continue to hold large endowments that could help write off the entire student debt in most countries. Yet, they continued to charge exorbitant and ever-increasing tuition fees from students. The net result was quite simple, the education that uplifted a person beyond poverty and might have even taken him/ her beyond being poor was now a noose around the person's neck. Pull too hard and try to break away from poverty and the burden of student debt will break your neck. Education has been weaponised even more now by the blue bloods than ever before. As jobs require higher levels of basic education even though not commensurate with the skill requirement of the job, the economics of education ensure that the poor shall remain poor.

Education has been touted as the way up for the masses – the path to riches. Yet, a vast majority of the population only stays poor even after being educated. Then, there are the politicians who speak of providing waiver on education loans – a mechanism they say will restore the balance. Yet, these politicians only help create a new imbalance – one between people who fell into the education trap and those who chose the walk their own path either by choice or because they could barely access credit. The idea being that a one-time waiver will reduce the burden and uplift some people beyond poverty while keeping the system intact. The state's responsibility to ensure equity by providing access to free universal education that makes a person both employable and empowered to rise beyond being poor continues to be shirked in the name of capitalism. If account were to be taken of the money wasted and funnelled to crony capitalists, the funding for universal education would be easy to find.

It is also ironic that these same politicians seek to target whom they call the ultra-rich or wealthy and mostly point to tech billionaires who broke away from the poor. These politicians choose not to point out the blue bloods who continue to seek favours from the state. The system of pointing to people who rise from the poor at the cost of protecting people who continue to plunder the state and the people only ensures that crony capitalism is reinforced and protected. Such politicians pretend to be the friends of the poor, supporters of the blue-collar workers and those that fight for union rights. They are only the people ensuring the status quo is retained by arranging for handouts and targeting those that broke away from being poor through their genius. Hating on Jeff Bezos or Mark Zuckerberg or Elon Musk is the way to restore power to the blue bloods who hide their fortunes in family trusts and through structures that ensure lobbying payments are made and campaign donations are made to the seamless well-oiled machine.

EDUCATION IS THE MOST WELL OILED SCAM THAT KEEPS THE POOR POOR BUT NOT POOR ENOUGH TO CAUSE A REBELLION. EDUCATION IS ACTUALLY THAT STATE OF ECONOMIC EQUILIBRIUM AND SOCIAL REST THAT ALLOWS CAPITALIST DEMOCRACIES TO FUNCTION IN A SELF-RIGHTEOUS MANNER.

Savings have long been touted as the way for the poor to secure their financial future. Savings not investments. The poor continue to save through years of work mostly into risk free instruments. Over the years and across geographies, interest rates have kept steadily declining and have, in many countries, hit zero or negative rates. This has ensured that the savings of the poor lose value not just through inflation but also by them not earning interest on their savings. Bank charges on holding savings accounts and depositing money have ballooned. Transacting on your own savings now costs more than it ever did. All this pushes the savings of the poor into one avenue – capital markets. Now, investments in capital markets are a good hedge against inflation. So, they are by their very nature not anti-poor. However, the scruples of players in the capital markets, especially those who can raise capital without accountability, it at best questionable.

Most people raising funds in capital markets represent the blue bloods and more recently the geniuses. While the blue bloods have been from time to time been dogged by accounting scams and keep the machinery well fed by paying the right price to auditors and rating agencies, they have little regard for longevity of their businesses that raise public money. Life span of listed organizations has been steadily declining which means even in capital markets, the odds are largely stacked against the poor investor. Now, add to this capital market scams, insider trading, market rigging, ponzi schemes and a dozen other methods of defrauding the poor investor, the odds are stacked against the poor investor.

Yet, while savings are the way to stay poor, astute investing offers some hope for the poor. The masses have had greater access to capital markets and financial education in recent times. However, they compete with Wall Street and many other such streets across the world who are firmly backed by and engaged in enhancing the value of the money that the blue bloods have accumulated over time. Even the tech geniuses by diluting to private equity are merely helping fuel a multiplication of wealth of the blue bloods.

SAVING FOR A RAINY DAY IS AN OLD ADAGE THAT ONLY HELPS KEEP THE STATUS QUO IN THE ECONOMICS OF MONEY

SUPPLY. IN MOST CASES, RAINY DAYS ONLY RAIN HARDER ON A POOR PERSON'S SAVINGS.

The poor do have a chance through investing their savings, but the odds are firmly stacked against them. Bankers have long been the tool of the blue bloods in their effort to protect their wealth. Savings only help count chickens while the eggs are hatching in the rich person's home.

CHAPTER 3
THE DOLLAR REMAINS KING

Chapter 3 – The dollar remains king

The economics of dollarization are the ultimate unholy grail towards globalizing the economics of money supply. The economics of money supply stayed localized for the longest time until capital convertibility came about. Capital convertibility still scares a number of central banks because, on record, it concerns them that it might lead to import of dollar inflation into their own economies. In reality, it is simply because they would like to run their own economics of money supply with greater control over who gets enriched.

With global trade the highest it has ever been, capital account convertibility constraints in a number of economics only ensures that they have greater control over unjust enrichment. It does not in any ways change the dynamics of their economy. It also allows central banks the opportunity to run economic cycles instead of aligning their economic cycles with the Federal Reserve. Now, why would they resist and simply not align if all central banks are seeking the same outcome. In certain countries, it may be difficult to justify bailouts to the rich. It is also difficult to sell the 'too big to fail theory' as they pride themselves on socialism and the power of the state. It conflicts with their narrative if they directly provide bailouts. So, if they can control the economic cycle and enable their rich to enter and exit at the right time, it helps them manage the narrative better. The other alternative for them, of course, is to let the rich default on loans taken in limited liability corporations away from their own assets. This has been the most popular tool for fiscal and monetary policy. Allowing the rich to default on loans with almost no repercussions whereas the poor are provided loan waivers selectively closer to elections has been a perfect tool for maintaining the status quo.

There lies one major problem with this sweet arrangement – global trade makes it imperative to either hold or freely convert the dollar. So, to manage this balance, central banks have come around with two alternatives: (i) keep large reserves i.e. hold the dollar (ii) peg or manage float against the dollar. The question has abounded and confounded many as to how and why central banks keep such large dollar reserves and pride themselves on the size of the reserves. Now, many countries take pride in their foreign currency reserves and holding of US Treasuries. The reality is that they are simply furthering the objective of using dollar reserves to re-align their economic cycles to the benefit of their crony capitalist. Reserves are merely a tool to balance the value of the dollar against their own currency. The tool is used only for a short-term until the central bank feels comfortable after engaging with the fiscal that the economic cycle can be reversed since the crony capitalists have made their dime. Any conflict between the central bank and government on the timing generally leads to removal or the central bank governors. It is a simple backstop governments exercise on the central bank which effectively aligns the timing of the economic cycle with the interest of their crony capitalists. Such disputes between central banks and governments are rare since most central bankers already understand that they are merely tools of the fiscal economic policies. Any ideologies about autonomy and freedom are just that – narratives for the general public – the poor who remain poor.

Now the second most effective tool is keeping a peg against the dollar or managing a float. Central banks already manipulate interest rates and money supply on behalf of the government and by corollary on behalf of the rich. Adding currency manipulation to their arsenal is not so much a tool of absolute control but timing of control. It is an oft asked question as to why a central bank was able to manage its currency value at one time and even with such large reserves is not able to manage it another time. The answer is simple – it doesn't want to. Because this time around it does not suit the timing of economic cycles for the rich. The manipulation of currency is key to managing economic cycles in-country mainly. In some cases, where countries are large exporters to the United States, the manipulation of currency through pegs impacts the US economy by pushing along consumerism when it is not aligned with the cyclical wishes of the US rich. This then allows for unjust enrichment of the rich in the country that exports to the US or countries with free capital account convertibility. Such manipulation beyond the scope of the original idea of using currency pegs is a dangerous territory some central banks have waded into.

The question is how does currency manipulation work and how does it lead to stealing from one country's rich for another country's rich. The answer is simple and takes the following steps:

- Send goods or services at a relatively lower value to countries and the earn their currency in return let's say the US Dollar.
- Keep the home currency pegged or manage the float by artificially depreciating it
- Use the dollars then to buy and hoard assets in the US especially when they are cheap in the US economic cycle
- Sell the US assets during the bubbles in the economic cycle in the US
- Remit the money back to the home country
- Depreciate the home country currency
- Buy assets in the home country cheap at the opposite end of the economic cycle
- Transfer the riches from the rich in US to the rich in another country
- The poor lose at both ends of the spectrum

Now, this is dangerous territory because it infringes on the holy position that central banks are universal common manipulators with the same set of objectives – mainly enriching the rich at the cost of the poor. When you steal from one country's rich, you are stealing from its central bank and retribution should be expected. Such retribution tends to be swift and brutal in the form of tariffs, sanctions, currency controls and general harassment in the trade cycle. This will continue until the status quo is replaced. Some countries central banks have believed that they can continue to lobby their way out of these problems and have been partially successful but eventually it catches on. In recent times, such countries have been labelled currency manipulators. In reality, it is a game of one upmanship where the art of manipulation should be limited to your own people and not others. Honour among thieves is critical to maintaining central banking activity globally.

Now why will the dollar remain king and why won't an offending central bank simply try to replace the USD with its own. The answer is simple – it would be stupid to do so. The dollar is an absolute store of value. Not really a currency. It is more a commodity that stores value. What that means is if you destroy the store of value, you destroy the value. If your try to replace the store of value with your own store, you open your own store to manipulation and destruction much like you did unto another.

The dollar retains its power as an absolute store of value as the currency peggers and manipulators need its longevity to keep their local narrative and wealth rebalancing systems alive. The real threat to the dollar dominance does not lie in another country's currency but it lies in the dollar itself losing its value as an absolute store of value. The easiest way to do this would be to make dollar a relative store of value.

The dollar becomes a relative store of value as soon as it is replaced by digital currencies or cryptos. These currencies create a cross border mechanism for trade replacing the dollar which means taking away the power of the Federal Reserve to rebalance wealth and by corollary taking away the power of all central banks to do the same. The easy answer then is to ban cryptos. However, the problem lies in the fact that central banks understand that if all you need is a store of value, a crypto is as useful as an online wallet and a PayPal account. All that is needed is to change its denomination from USD to a virtual currency let's say tokens or virtual coins or points. And suddenly a new store of value has emerged. An absolute store of value that makes the USD a relative store of value and no longer an absolute store of value that can be manipulated by central banks.

Most central banks have recognized the inevitable and are seeking to launch their own digital currencies. Currencies they can continue to manipulate to restore the balance of wealth the way they like.

CRYPTOS THREATEN THE VERY EXISTENCE OF THE ECONOMICS OF MONEY SUPPLY AND DOLLARIZATION. WHILE THEY ARE IMPERFECT AND AS SUSECPTIBLE TO MAINPULATION, THEY TRANSFER POWER FROM THE HANDS OF A SINGLE MAINPULATOR TO MANY.

Cryptos are likely to get dollarized as legislation and innovation by governments and central banks hastens the demise of the existing ones and seeks their replacement with centrally manipulated ones. Yet, cryptos offer a ray of hope to take the power away from the manipulators. The reason for the cryptos getting dollarized will not in the end be because of central bank innovation or legislation. It will be because people need a power to tell them what is right. The power does not have to be correct or honest, it just has to be more visible. Demonizing big tech is furthering the narrative of central banks and governments to ensure that no one is more visible and recognizable than them. Talking of breaking up big tech because they are too powerful is simply a narrative to ensure that big tech does not replace the balance of wealth by issuing more recognizable currency.

CHAPTER 4
EVERYTHING GETS CONSUMED OR HOARDED BEFORE IT TRICKLES DOWN

Chapter 4 – Everything gets consumed or hoarded before it trickles down

The fundamental narrative in support of the economics of money supply is trickle-down economics. It simply means that if you put money in a funnel, it will eventually find its way to the bottom. The analogy may be true except that central banks do not put money in funnels. They put money in leaky pipes and more importantly rusted pipes.

Central banks put money primarily into the banking system. A fraction of that money is put into direct benefit transfer schemes to the poor. A large proportion compared to what is put in the banking systems is spent on infrastructure and other investment projects of the government. Now, what does this mean to the poor man. Money put into the banking system will only be lent on to the rich – the poor are simply not credit worthy. The direct benefit transfers, if any, will be one cheque in the mail that may help reduce stress for a month or two. Large investments in infrastructure of other government projects will be awarded to the rich who will fund these with loans from the banks. So, in simple terms two leaky rusted pipes will carry wealth to the rich whereas one heavily controlled and trickling pipe will carry a little money to the poor. Now why leaky? It has to leak so that the politicians, by whatever name called and whatever philosophy they seek to further, are paid their share of the leakage. The share does not have to be exorbitant because they do not seek money. They simply seek to retain power into perpetuity. What does a poor man get in the trickle-down economics – a job if the leakage is lesser or a few hand-outs if the leakage is larger. The degree of leakage from the leaky pipes determines how poor the poor shall be. The degree of leakage may reduce or increase in different governmental regimes. However, the leakage is an essential part of the system. It keeps the powerful motivated to transfer wealth to the rich.

LEAKY PIPES AND NARROW FUNNELS ARE THE WAY TO ENSURE THAT TRICKLE-DOWN ECONOMICS DOESN'T ALLOW TOO MUCH TRICKLE DOWN AND THREATEN THE ENTIRE SYSTEM OF MONEY SUPPLY ECONOMICS

Now a simple question arises – if central banks can simply print money, why not just print more and let it trickle freely. It would help the rich get richer and the poor also rich. It is not that simple. The money supply has to eventually buy assets because the money itself loses value with every new printing. The diminution in value may or may not be reflected immediately. Now, if there is too much money chasing too few assets, it becomes difficult for the rich to buy the assets to retain the value of their loot. If there are more assets created, then the assets themselves will lose value thereby making the unjust enrichment process self-defeating. Hence, regulating money supply is an important role of the central bank. Central bankers will throw jargon like M2, M3 and the like at you to try to explain they are doing something very important. In reality, they are simply ensuring that money trickles down to the poor and gushes to the rich. If too much is trickling down as opposed to gushing to the rich, it is important to either redirect the money by modifying monetary policy or simply printing less to ensure that assets retain their value.

Keynesian economics speaks of the concept of investments to create a multiplier in the economy. It works on a simple assumption that more you put into the hands of people the more they are likely to save or consume which will get invested and then help multiply growth. Now, there are two major problems with this – (i) the more you put in the hands of people, the more they consume or save is incorrect. Beyond a point, they simply hoard. Either they hoard by buying assets or hoard the cash itself for future consumption. (ii) people are generalized as all people. People inherently rich only see the money as a way to enrich themselves and enjoy consumption like never before. Poor people on the other hand see the money as a rainy-day store. In simple terms, money will get hoarded or consumed before it trickles down. The quantum of investment is not driven by the quantum of money printed or supplied, it is simply driven by the avenues provided by the government and the economics of leakage. The greater the government spend or policy allocation, the greater the investment and the greater the multiplier. Printing currency in the absence of a corresponding fiscal spending plan simply leads to consumerism or hoarding. No trickle down and no multiplier. Most fiscal spending plans rarely coincide with central bank monetary expansion. Hence, trickle down economics only support consumerism and hoarding not investments.

THE ECONOMICS OF MONEY SUPPLY, JUSTIFIED THROUGH THE LENS OF TRICKLE- DOWN ECONOMICS, IS AS SLOW AND EXCURCIATING TO WATCH AS WATCHING A THIRSTY PERSON STRUGGLE FOR THE FEW DROPS OF WATER ONLY REALIZE IT IS THEIR OWN SWEAT, THEY ARE DRINKING. TRICKLE DOWN ECONOMICS CREATES A DESPERATELY POORER SOCIETY.

To ensure that people do not die from drinking their own sweat, trickle down economics also has the provision for lending credit and liquidity to the poor from time to time. Governments propagate this through loans for small businesses, start-ups and other small employment creators. More importantly, direct consumer loans are provided to help with consumption economics. All these sources of liquidity are predatory. The fact still remains that while every expected credit loss model suggested that chunky corporate loans are riskier than loans to small business or consumers, small businesses and consumers continue to pay obscene rates of interest. At these rates, a bank's money lent will typically double in 3-4 years, compounding and all. While loans to large businesses primarily owned by the bluebloods adjusted for credit losses will yield negative returns for the banks. These negative returns are funded by positive returns from consumer credit or in case where banks do not hold this corporate credit and securitize it, this credit finds its way back into the pensions of poor people. Either ways, the banks ensure that trickle down economics finds an additional method to keep the poor poorer.

CHAPTER 5
CENTRAL BANKS ARE KEY TO STRENGTHENING THE ILLUSION THAT THERE EXISTS BALANCE AND INTEGRITY IN FINANCIAL MARKETS

Chapter 5 – Central banks are key to furthering the illusion that there exists balance and integrity in financial markets

Now, before you start thinking that everything described herein is a conspiracy theory – it isn't. It is neither a true nor a false conspiracy theory. It is a system. A system developed and perfected over years. A system that works like clockwork sometimes not even realizing its purpose or the fact that it causes unjust enrichment. It is a system that pre-dates true democracy and was built on capitalism without the security provided to capital today. A system that was designed to protect the rich and mainly to protect capital. It is a system that was built for a different era and simply carried forward into the current era. The system works and it has worked for many decades and in some cases centuries to further the goals of capitalism. It has metamorphosed itself with communism, socialism and autocracy in a way that makes it very sustainable. And the reason it has survived so many different regimes, philosophies and thought processes is because it appeals to the innate human sensibility. The sensibility that wants security or the perception of security for itself irrespective of who manipulates what beyond the realm of oneself. To be sure, though, that such manipulation is not seen as determinantal or not seen at all, you have central banks and more recently financial market regulators. Their primary job is to promulgate and further strengthen the system whether they realize it or not. Their job is to simply ensure that the status quo continues. Because the status quo keeps the system working for its original intended objective.

Central banks are key to furthering the illusion that there exists equity, justice and balance in financial markets. What exists is merely a status quo, an attempt to keep the market in the same place. Any innovation can be allowed if it ensures status quo in the market. Most innovations in financial markets, therefore, happen outside the ambit of regulation. Regulators, then, clamp down very stoically on such innovation by regulating it or shutting it down. Regulating it simply means aligning it back with the status quo – creating an illusion that innovation has happened but ensuring the original methods are retained. Where alignment cannot happen, the enterprise and with it the innovation will be shut down. The smarter regulators are more tolerant and understand that regulating is better than shutting it down. An idea once born does not truly shut down but will simply operate in a different ecosystem. An idea moulded to the old school is a better death knell for any disruption that idea was conceived with. All other talks of disruption in financial markets are not innovations but merely disaggregation of financial services caused by more efficient ways to deliver the same old. The only innovation in financial services over the years has been reduction in head count by replacing humans with technology. That is called disruption by central banks and regulators alike. It does not replace the current system or come close to even changing its ways. It only strengthens the system and its operating methods by cementing it with machines in place of humans. In effect, all innovation in financial services is making the economics of money supply even less human than it always was.

Over the years, central banks and regulators have found ways to regulate the market they say is in public interest. Regulate the way people issue, trade, or provide services to the broader investor base. One of the biggest areas in which transparency has apparently improved is disclosure of financial statements – demonstrating to people whose money is taken either in the form of debt or equity what is being done with that money. However, those rules of accounting and disclosure do not apply to governments. Ironically, governments, government agencies, departments and enterprises floated by the government are the largest borrowers in financial markets. While most enterprises are subject to the same level of reporting as private enterprises, they are regularly and freely accorded exceptions in the guise of greater good. The government itself though borrows freely with the least amount of oversight and accountability. This is not limited to the US Government. This is the universal truth across governments. If only the accounting standards and auditing standards were applied to the governments, it would become clear that central banks and regulators have facilitated extrication of money from poor people to funnel to the governments and in turn to the rich. While the rich pay less taxes per dollar in most countries through structuring and other means, they also indirectly borrow money from poor people through government borrowing programs. The illusion of transparency and integrity applies only to private enterprises. In reality, the largest borrower is exempt from any transparency.

WHEN THE LARGEST BORROWER IN FINANCIAL MARKETS CAN OPERATE UNABATED THROUGH LEGISLATION, ANY TRANSPARENCY AND GOVERNANCE ENFORCED THEREAFTER CAN ONLY BE SEEN AS HYPOCRSIY TO EYEWASH THE OBVIOUS EXTRICATION OF A POOR PERSON'S WEALTH

Allowing central banks to earn seigniorage over and above the open thievery by governments is a further slander on the illusion of balance in financial markets. Seigniorage is simply the difference in value of the currency the central bank prints and the cost of printing it. Each year, this difference is passed back to governments through dividends, accumulations and other forms of transfer. Not only does the largest borrower have access to people's money unabated, but it also rubs salt into the wounds of the poor by earning seigniorage. All this money, one must not forget, finds its way to the blue-blooded in the name of tax breaks, investments, grants and other methods of transfer that ensure the rich stay rich.

CHAPTER 6
IS IT ALL GLOOM AND DOOM FOR THE POOR?

Chapter 6 – Is it all gloom and doom for the poor?

The system is so deeply rooted across the world that it isn't even intentional thievery anymore. It is just a way of life. A philosophy that seems fair because there isn't an alternative. Some alternatives are being cultivated in the Scandinavian countries and start with simple fundamentals. Basic changes in the economic structure, though small, can have lasting impacts on removing the rich-poor divide. The economics of money supply and dollarization, though not abolishable immediately, can be watered down with getting other basics right. The agenda for change should be at least cover the following:

- Universal health is a good way to ensure that the poor have protection against vagaries and don't slip into the abyss. Universal health, while purported to cost a lot, can simply be managed by printing money like is done for many other causes.
- Universal education at least up unto a person is employable is necessary. Education has to be free and a fundamental right of citizens. Universal education should cover not just degrees but also skilling. Ensuring that public education is as effective as private education is critical to restoring the balance.
- Pricing of credit has to become universally visible to all. Banks and financial institutions should be able to demonstrate and be audited to prove that the price at which they lent to the poor was not exploitative. More importantly, they should be able to prove that the pricing of credit was always commensurate with the risk of the borrower and such risk is not assessed by internal models but clear and transparent benchmarks.
- The government balance sheet covering the balance sheet of each and every one of its departments should be subjected to the same standards of accounting and auditing applicable to private enterprises. The government owes an explanation for every dollar spent and this explanation cannot be in the form of clandestine budgets hidden away in the name of national

security or national secrets. It should be able to explain to its citizens how it spent the citizens money and why it has run deficits on their funds.
- Baseline for services expected in return for taxes is required. Tax is a quid pro quo relationship. Economists who try to say it isn't are simply covering for the government. Tax is an amount paid in return for a service. Much like private enterprises, governments need to be upfront and clear about what services are provided in return for taxes. The services so provided can be run by the government or purchased by the government from private enterprises on behalf of the government. Either way, the baseline for services must be disclosed and the actual provision of service against the baseline tracked.

The debate is not between capitalism or socialism. It is not been democracy or autocracy. It is a simple issue of accountability and providing the service for which government's charge you. Governments should not be beyond reproach and question. This is the first step to restoring the balance between the rich and the poor. There is no other fair method of providing reparations. It is time to make a fresh start and correct the divide here on in.

www.ingramcontent.com/pod-product-compliance
Lightning Source LLC
Chambersburg PA
CBHW050319220526
45465CB00005B/2046